"Spiritual Living Waters"

Flowing in Words

By

Christina R Jussaume

©2008 by Christina R Jussaume
All rights reserved. No part of this book may be reproduced, stored in a retrieval system or transmitted in any form by any means without the prior permission of the publishers, except by a reviewer who may quote brief passages in a review to be printed in a newspaper, magazine or journal.
IBSN: 978-0-6151-8873-7

Newly Created Poetry Forms

By

Christina R Jussaume

&****&

هشش Ö ششم

Feeling His love
(Candlelight)

Know spiritual cup
He will lift you up
Know he walks beside
Feelings can't hide
Give him your trust
This is must
Behold
Jesus
Within
He
Will
Calm
You
When
You
Need
Respect his guidance always.

&****&

Rebirth (Tree of Life)

Tree
Is the
Rebirth of
All on the earth
It must be cared for
If cared for, it will thrive
If neglected, it will die
The trunk will show number of years
It depends on the rain and the sun
Their seeds will then spread when the winds blow strong
With maintenance the seedlings will then flourish
We must preserve the forests never polluting
If all of this is done, tree of life will multiply
The trunk widens
It becomes strong
It stands quite strong
It's like anchor
Holding unto
All life's values

&****&

Table of Contents   Page 1

Christina Crj147 (Acrostic)	Page 11
Legend of Donkey's Cross (Cascade)	Page 13
Acceptance (Rondelet)	Page 14
The Mountain Chapel (English Sonnet)	Page 15
Embrace God's Love (Christ-in-a-Rhyme)	Page 16
Conquering Fear (Jewels Rule)	Page 17
Tribute to Parents (Joseph's Star)	Page 18
The Beautiful Hummingbirds (Wrapped Refrain)	Page 20
The Heavens (Constanza)	Page 21
Paws of Love (Quatrain)	Page 22
Granddaughter (Acrostic)	Page 24
Our Destiny (Patricia's Harmony)	Page 25
Grandson (Acrostic)	Page 26
The Wildlife Reserve (Haiku/Senryu)	Page 27
The Landscaper's Vision (English Pensee)	Page 28
Baby Steps (Monchielle)	Page 29
Angel Voices Loud and Clear (Quatrain)	Page 30
Daughter (Rictameter)	Page 32
Beacon of Hope (Shaped Poetry)	Page 34
Everlasting & Serenity (8 x 4)	Page 35
If We Had One More Day with Deceased	Page 36
Comfort (Acrostic/chain/senryu)	Page 37
Appreciation (Free verse)	Page 38
Marriage Blessings (Monetetra)	Page 40
The Golden Rule (Pentaphor)	Page 42
Butterfly (Butterfly)	Page 44
The Albino Peacock (Cascade)	Page 45
The Earth (Cascade)	Page 46
The Gift of Using Words (Choka)	Page 48
Paws of Love Part 2 (Quatrain)	Page 49
Christina's Choices (English Sonnet)	Page 50
Living in God's Image (Crown Oddquain)	Page 52
Jesus Speaks (Diatelle)	Page 53
Effects of Spiritual Waters (Triplets)	Page 54
For all Lonely People (Tetratyctys)	Page 55
Relativity of Time (English Pensee)	Page 56
Forgiveness (Michelle's Heart)	Page 57

Table of Contents Page 2

Wildflower Meadows (Cascade)	Page 58
The Good Neighbor (French Rhyme Royal)	Page 60
The Promised Land (Nonet/Rictameter/Senryu)	Page 61
The Peacemakers (English Sonnet)	Page 62
God speaks Through Me (Somonka)	Page 63
Poetry (Shandorma)	Page 64
God's Creation (Tanka)	Page 65
Philosophy of Life (ABC Senryu)	Page 66
Guardian Angels (Seventh Heaven)	Page 68
A Week in Time (Seventh Heaven)	Page 69
My Christmas Wish (English Sonnet)	Page 70
God's Blessings (Senryu)	Page 71
This Poet's Reflection (English Sonnet)	Page 72
Valentines Day (Acrostic)	Page 73
Christmas Season (ABC Two Word Acrostic)	Page 74
Angelic Intervention (Nonet/Senryu)	Page 75
Spiritual Healers (Sonnet/Quatrain)	Page 76
ABC Two Word Acrostic	Page 78
The Ark (Freeverse)	Page 80
Golden Rule (Quatrain)	Page 81
My Rainbow (English Sonnet)	Page 82
Thunder in the Heavens (English Sonnet)	Page 83
Heaven on Earth (English Sonnet)	Page 84
Perseverance (Acrostic)	Page 85
Prayer for Reduction of Stress	Page 86
Prayer for Asthmatics (Christ-in-a-Rhyme)	Page 87
Crisp Autumn Air (Luckyleaf)	Page 88
Christmas Acrostics	Page 89
Happy New Year(Acrostic/Senryu)	Page 90
God's advice to all (Abc Darien)	Page 92
A Kodak Moment (Cascade)	Page 93
My Feelings on my Death (Quatrain)	Page 96
Prayer for Retirees (Christ-in-a-Rhyme)	Page 97
Life (Quatrain)	Page 98

Table of Contents Page 3

The Aquatic Plants (Haiku/Senryu)	Page 100
Chariots of Fire (Quatrain)	Page 102
Locks of Love (Quatrain)	Page 103
Open Invitation of God (Christ-in-a-Rhyme)	Page 104
Morning Beginnings (Cascade)	Page 105
The Lilac (Monorhyme)	Page 106
My Soul's Flight (Candlelight)	Page 107
Chariots of Fire Part 2 (Quatrain)	Page 108
God's Blessings (Challenge Poem)	Page 109
The Invitation (Kyrielle)	Page 110
Angel Kisses (Luckyleaf)	Page 111
The Poet and the Artist (English Sonnet)	Page 112
The Blessed Trinity (Quatrain)	Page 113
My Vision (Quatrain)	Page 114
Chariots of Fire Part 3 (Quatrain)	Page 115
Light of the World (Candlelight)	Page 116
The Timetable of God (Kyrielle Sonnet)	Page 117
Eternal Life Promised (Christ-in-a-Rhyme)	Page 118
A Day I'll Treasure (English Sonnet)	Page 119
Effects of Jealousy (Michelle's Heart)	Page 120
Mustard Seed of Faith (Swap Quatrain)	Page 121
My Bright White Star (Quatrain)	Page 122
My King (Tina-Rhyme)	Page 124
Holy Spirit (Pentaphor)	Page 125
Jesus Has Risen (Monchielle)	Page 126
Hopes and Dreams (Italian Sonnet)	Page 128
Summer's Beauty (English Sonnet)	Page 129
The Fall Portrait (Haiku/Senryu)	Page 130
Tree Rings (Haiku/Senryu)	Page 133
The Fireflies (Haiku/Senryu)	Page 134
Envy (Tetratryctys)	Page 135
My Muse (Choka)	Page 137
Essence (Monorhyme)	Page 137
Love Shared (English Cameo)	Page 138
Believing in Jesus (Rictameter)	Page 139

Dedication

My Husband, Daughter and Grandchildren

&**&**

Author Acknowledgments

This collection is inspired by God, my family and all the poets that gave me challenges to write on different subjects. Within this collection, I have used many types of poetic forms. I have created two new forms myself. I have a poetic glossary in the back of the book that explains all the forms that I did use in this collection and the inventors of each new form.

I would like to thank all the poets that have helped me by continually challenging me to write on various subjects and sometimes in various formats. They all have read my poems on sites that I belong to and have helped me to become the poet that I am. I will attempt to write on any subject that I am familiar with, as long as the material I write is uplifting in nature. I believe God gave me this ability to help comfort others with the words that I do write.

Christina Crj147
(Acrostic)

Christ is the first six letters of my name
His spirit is within me until he does reclaim
Realize he should be first in your life
In doing so, you feel less pressure when in strife
Sins need to be repented and you will feel free
Trade the devil for Jesus and revelation you see
Inspiration from God gives me wisdom to write
Necessary to live in his image, is my insight
Always believe he will return to bring us delight

&****&

Christian woman hoping to write to please others
Remember to write for all sisters and brothers
Just as he has spoken, love and honor all Mothers

&****&

1 One time only to live my life
4 Four times God gave seasons to relieve strife
7 Seven times I'll say make each day count in life

&****&

Legend of Donkey's Cross

Small donkeys have a cross on back
Mary did ride to Bethlehem
She bore Jesus in a stable
There had been no room at the inn

&****&

Donkeys were used to travel then
Owners found them affectionate
They were fed grass and also hay
Small donkeys have a cross on back

&****&

Their lifetime is quite a long while
They can live over thirty years
Jesus was brought up with donkey
Mary did ride to Bethlehem

&****&

Donkey did love him as Master
He stayed with him when crucified
Sun's shadow left a cross on back
She bore Jesus in a stable

&****&

Even today they have a cross
The humblest animal God loves
Remember this when you see one
There had been no room at the inn

&****&

Acceptance

Accept Jesus
Welcome him into your heart now
Accept Jesus
It is through him we become whole
He watches us from up above
He cares for us with his great love
Accept Jesus

&****&

Let him guide you
Listen to your inner spirit
Let him guide you
He's with you in good times and bad
He wants you to make right choices
Listen close to angel voices'
Let him guide you

&****&

The Mountain Chapel

The mountain chapel gave us a great view
Sometimes swans could be seen swimming in peace.
It was by the cobblestone bridge all knew.
Inside everyone would pray all wars cease.

&****&

On a foggy morn the mountains were seen
It was a welcome to see such a sight
As the sun rose, the river looked pristine.
God's beauty was there to give all delight.

&****&

On the bridge sometimes at dusk, some would fish.
The sunset would reflect bringing a glow.
They carried fish home for wife to make dish.
A couple would walk by extremely slow.

&****&

All attended here in friendship and love.
They praised God and looked up to him above.

&****&

Embrace God's Love

Embrace Holy Spirit within
Keep away from unneeded sin
When doing this you surely win

&****&

God's presence helps in whatever you may attempt to do
Follow his example and your life will always be true
He watches hoping more accept him beside me and you

&***&

He can calm a raging storm
He is with your child at dorm
He can help you to feel warm

&****&

He is caring God
He is King and Lord
He's on path I trod

&***&

Believe he is love
He watches above
Gives of peace of dove

&****&

Conquering Fear
(Jewels Rule)

Conquer all fear

Let us know that you are near

Help us to choose the right door,

Forevermore

Safe we must feel

Need not worry of next meal

We pray that help you will give

Please let us live

Please show us way

This is what we do now pray

We read your Bible each night

Please give insight

&****&

*Creator Chazz Combs

Tributes to Parents
(Joseph's Star)

Dad
I do miss
I think of our love
I fall back on memories
I know your together now
I have no sadness
For now I
Write

&****&

�هششهӦششه

Mom
I love you
I feel your presence
I know you are real happy
You are in paradise now
You tend God's gardens
On bended
Knee

&****&

I
Hear angels
You are both among
Mom greets the new arrivals
Dad escorts them to meet God
As Daughter I'm proud
To be your
Seed

&****&

Now
I must wait
God helps me with verse
I write to praise Holy name
Both of your are guardians
I cherish you both
Forever
Yours

&****&

The Beautiful Hummingbirds

The hummingbirds are quite pretty.
They're seen in country or city.
They are so extremely tiny.
They are attracted to things shiny.
They are the most delicate of all kinds of birds.
Distinct chirping is known for all the hummingbirds.

&****&

Their many hues can be quite bright.
Watching them is a pleasant sight.
They hover in mid-air near bloom.
The praying mantis is their doom.
Their activity can help most of us with blues.
They're like an artist palette with their many hues.

&****&

Most of the males are aggressive.
They are also quite possessive.
Females will tolerate others.
Babies will stay close to Mothers.
Males fly into other males and then one prevails.
Fighting often occurs among most of the males.

&****&

The Heavens

The moon glows brightly on dark night
All crops are planted by the moon
Watering is done by monsoon

&****&

It is romantic pretty sight
Lovers find it casts a great spell
Passionate emotions do swell

&****&

The stars blink brightly with delight
A shooting star flies by real fast
Watching it you hoped it would last

&***&

Stars are little angels in flight
Peace overcomes me as I view
I feel as if seen one I knew

&***&

Viewing the moon shows us God's might
Land, sea, and heavens created
All of us should be elated!

&***&

Paws of Love
(Quatrain)

Perennial garden is in front of their yard.
Spectacular view would be good in a nice card.
The plants have many different colors to delight.
From roadside; it gives all a memorable sight.

&****&

There were many lawn ornaments inside to view.
I saw many critters and a gazing ball too.
Couple worked together to bring out its glory.
She showed me all with pride; and this is her story.

&***&

Some varieties came from bulbs that they did plant.
As some flowers were in bloom, the view did enchant.
Others had been a gift from one of her kind friends.
Sometimes cuttings do not work; it really depends.

&****&

They did love their garden that they toiled together.
They were thankful for it in all kinds of weather.
Lynn made garden stone with a mold of a huge paw.
There were paw prints all around, what beauty I saw.

&****&

Hard work really does pay off, and now they enjoy.
I hope there is nothing that ever does destroy.
Now they sit on their porch, and see its great beauty.
They will keep all weeds out as it is their duty.

&****&

&****&

Granddaughter
(Acrostic)

Granddaughter was delight to spend time with
Reached out to me, with love she had to give
Also made me feel great; that I belonged to her
Never did she stop asking me, of how things were
Did enjoy me playing with her, with her small doll
Did not mind I did not feel like playing with ball
Always liked to hug and show that she did care
Usually liked playing out getting some fresh air
Good girl did make her Grandmother very happy
Hilarious to be with; we often got real sappy
Together entire day and time just flew on by
Eventually, had to bring home with a sigh
Remembering the heights; I soared so very high

&****&

Our Destiny

Patience is needed
Always know that God's in charge
Try to understand

&****&

Renew your values
In stressful times do keep calm
Christ is always there

&****&

Inner spirit guides
Always listen to message
Soul will feel lighter

&****&

Hear the angel's sing
Almighty God is with them
Realize your goal

&***&

Many times trials will be a test
Omnipotent Lord knows what's best
Never let your faith dwindle down
Yearn to feel his love turn around

*Patricia's Harmony

&****&

Grandson
(Acrostic)

Grandson loves to watch Superman
Ready to view and understand
Action scenes hold interest well
Needs to watch again and then tell
Delights in the computer games
Seriously knows all their names
Often beats his sister in score
Needed Grandson I adore

&****&

The Wildlife Reserve

Serene Park reserve
All animals here are safe
Here they breed freely

&****&

There are nature walks
Birdwatchers see many kinds
They bring cameras

&****&

Deer live in these woods
There is a stream where they drink
There are many oaks

&****&

Squirrel gather nuts
They bury for harsh winter
Holes are everywhere

&****&

Park rangers patrol
They make sure they're no poachers
All wildlife is safe

&****&

God gave them this home
They survive hard times ahead
It is will of God

&****&

The Landscaper's Vision

Gardens,
Give us pleasure.
They give us feeling of peace.
Birds and butterflies are present.
Fragrance is in the air.

&****&

Valleys,
Have wildflowers.
They sprout up in the moist soil.
Bees and butterflies pollinate.
Flowers sway with the breeze.

&****&

Man-made,
Ponds have plant life.
Aquatic plants help the fish.
They give pond a colorful look.
Koi fish might reside here.

&****&

Pine trees,
Have a great scent.
Woodsy scent is pleasurable.
Cones are decorative also.
They give us a great view.

&****&

Baby Steps

Baby steps can help you
Set a goal to achieve
Do a little each day
You will accomplish it
It is the only way

&****&

Baby steps can help you
Do not think of long hours
Just imagine your goal
Do make yourself a plan
You will start to feel whole

&****&

Baby steps can help you
Great things require effort
Do use your talents well
Realize benefits
Then this advice you'll tell

&****&

Baby steps can help you
All projects start with them
Your wisdom is the best
You'll be happy when done
Patience did pass the test

&***&

Baby steps can help you
We all started like this
Recall your early years
See how far you have come
Now you shed joyful tears

&****&

Angel Voices Loud and Clear

Angel voices loud and clear
Singing praise of God always near
Children learning about God
On path of light, they will trod

&****&

Children file into church pew
All will accept host that's new
Little girls in pretty dress
They did repent and confess

&****&

Little boys all dressed in white
These couples were a delight
They do sing for all us there
Small angels of God aware

&****&

Angel voices we all hear
The songs they sing all dear
They sing of God and his love
Blessings sent down from above

&****&

Let them leave this church anew
With God within their not blue
Let heir faces show a glow
All will see Jesus and know

&****&

Daughter

Daughter
Intelligent
Aggressive, honest, kind
My closest friend and confident
Good Mother, Daughter and also fine wife
She is blessing in my life
Pretty and creative
Awesome person
Daughter

&****&

Precious
I love her so
We have hard time talking
Communicate better in verse
I keep away as her words only hurt
God give me strength to change for her
I hate when she compares
She'll always be
Precious

&****&

Unique
Molded by God
I obey all he tells
He awoke giving book's title
I am commanded by him to reach out
Sweetheart I must obey Jesus
Know that I love you lots
My love's within
Unique

&****&

Beacon of Hope

```
         _/\_
        /___\
       /_____\
      |_____|
))))))))))))))^(((((((((((((((
 )))))))))))))!(((((((((((((
```
\#Beacon of hope#
\#Given to cope#
\#Shines so bright#
Throughout the night
|_____|
\#All sailing the ocean#
\#Get tense with motion#
\#They look for the guiding light#
They shout out when they see sight
|_____|
\#Angelic light shows them their path#
\#\#They will not longer feel sea's wrath##
\#\#\#\#Calmness felt by all on the ship####
\#\#Now their face does not feel wind's whip##
|_____|
\#\#The lighthouse is now within their view####
They knew patience, God would see them through
\#\#\#They had got out of harm's way just in time###
|_____|
\#\#\#\#Waves were crashing now and hard to define###
\#\#\#Their families prayed they would not be harmed###
\#\#\#\#\#Now all shipmates were no longer alarmed#####
\#\#\#\#\#They would rest easier being moored here#####
\#They would share stories with lighthouse keeper so dear#
<<<<<<<<<<<<<<<<<<<<<<>>>>>>>>>>>>>>>>>>>>

*The lighthouse shape was created by a poet friend named Claire Saeger. The actual poem was my own words.

&****&

Everlasting

Everlasting
Will be our soul
That will take flight
From our body
Arrive in front
Of Heaven's gate
To mingle then
Among angels

&****&

Serenity

Serenity
We will all feel
When accepting
Our Savior's gift
Of Eternal
Everlasting
Tranquility
Within
Heaven

&***&

*Eight by Four (8 x 4) Syllable Sentence

This form was created by Alvin Othto Stewart. © 2007

If We Had One More Day with Deceased

My Mom would be the one that would be my choice.
In twenty-one years I have not heard her voice.
I often think of her, and I feel here near.
She was a great Mother, and I found her dear.

&****&

I would show her all we planted in the yard.
The two plum trees in the front were only hard.
She never knew I liked to see flowers grow.
We add a few things each year, and they grow slow.

&****&

She would meet her Great Grandchildren never seen.
They would not fear her knowing she was not mean.
A baked stuffed lobster I would make sure she had.
She did love that so much and I would feel glad.

&****&

Canasta and Scrabble I would play with her.
I hear her laughter with fun that would occur.
Michelle and Mom would play a game of Uno.
They got so silly, someone would have to go.

&****&

I would hug her and bring photos out to share.
When she had to leave us, she knew we did care.
I believe she watches all that she did love.
I feel she smiles down on me from up above.

&****&

Comfort

Comfort with the words that do heal
Oppose no one, rather appeal
Most of the time, hug those you meet
Foes forgive, rather than repeat
On other's problems, please listen
Realize why the stars glisten
Try to lead life of good Christian

&****&

Christian that gives praise
Praise of our dear Lord
Lord mold as desired
Desired and content
Content with spirit
Spirit does guide all
All listen real well
Well of life for all
All will never thirst
Thirst you will not know
Know Jesus within
Within heart and soul

&****&

Comfort all you can
You will feel joy doing this
This is Christian way

&****&

Appreciation

Appreciation is to value a person well.
They treat each other with respect and you can then tell.
In a marriage they both know this, and then let it show.
Their love can be seen in their eyes that really do glow.

&****&

They cherish all the great times they do spend together.
They are happy in any kind of drastic weather.
Their love remains as long as they understand treasure.
Each is a prize they will keep forever and ever.

&****&

Appreciate well
God gives us many blessings
Treasure each new day

&****&

Cherish the heavens
Gaze at the moon and bright stars
Feel warmth of the sun

&****&

Understand value
Do accept the plan of God
God is greatest prize!

&****&

Marriage Blessings

May your love ripen and bloom well
Do remember your wedding bell
Feel the love and laughter and tell
Home's in a dell, home's in a dell

&****&

Never go to bed being mad
Always find something to be glad
Someday hope you'll be a fine Dad
Do not buy fad, do not buy fad

&****&

May good health be with you all year
Let your marriage be always dear
Let there be a minimal tear
Conquer your fear, conquer your fear

&***&

Treasure memories you do share
Always tell each other you care
In each other's eyes you'll be fair
Waste not on dare, waste not on dare

&****&

The Golden Rule

Follow golden rule
Do what you want done
Be a friend to all
Do not prejudice
Be good example

&****&

**Never hold grudge
Forgive we must
Forget you're hurt
Begin anew**

&**&**

**Try harder
You'll succeed
It is great**

&**&**

**Your heart
Will feel**

&**&**

Light

&**&**

Butterfly

Supreme butterfly,
Flutter your wings,
Delicate
Beauty
Gliding
To feed
On blossom
Of my purple
Tall butterfly bush.

&****&

You are just gorgeous
A creation
Made by God
For all
Of us
To share
The monarch,
Spectacular
Black and orange hue.

&****&

*Butterfly--- Form created by Michael Degenhardt

The Albino Peacock

The male peacock saw a female
She was beautiful but all white
She pranced around within his view
He decided to pursue her

&****&

She did indeed enjoy his attention
Life would be harder with her white
Predators could easily see
The male peacock saw a female

&****&

In winter she would be real safe
He would be obvious to see
Their young would be very pretty
She was beautiful but all white

&****&

He would protect her in the spring
In winter she would be on guard
They would enjoy companionship
She pranced around within his view

&****&

Their young would love all peacocks met
They know how happy parents are
They would know its inside that counts
He decided to pursue her

&****&

The Earth

Our earth was created by God
He created mountains and seas
Babbling brooks were formed in valleys
Trees and wildflowers adorn it
The seas could be used for fishing
He created wildlife for all

&****&

The earth has an ecosystem
If humans take care, it will last
He gave us a sun to warm us
He gave us a moon to highlight night
Stars he placed in the sky to view
Our earth was created by God

&****&

He gave us days to tell time span
Sunday was a day we should rest
Four seasons he gave us pleasure
Each has things to look forward to
Winter gives time for family
He created mountains and seas

&****&

Sledding on frozen hills was fun
Igloos could be made to play in
When cold enough, ice skating too
Thermos of hot cocoa we drank
Spring brought color to our great earth
Babbling brooks were formed in valleys

&****&

Now families tend to gardens
Soil will grow us fine food with care
Children ride bikes up and down street
Many bird breeds are seen flying
Boats are moored to the docks at sea
Trees and wildflowers adorn it

&****&

Summer and fall brought us joy too
Summer brought barbecues and beach
Fall trees wear hats of many hues
Squirrels hoard their nuts for winter
Glimpses of wildlife you may see
The seas could be used for fishing

&****&

God gave us an earth with beauty
The weather gave us change of pace
Rain replenished the ground soil
Sun gave us warmth on a cold day
World beauty is a gift from God
He created wildlife for all

&****&

The Gift of Using Words

Words fascinate me
I am sure you all agree
Words have great power

&****&

They help to uplift
They show our expression well
They are poet's gift

&****&

Some have dual meaning
Take care in how you use them
They can heal or hurt

&****&

They give imagery
Images are beautiful
They show emotion

&***&

Wisdom can also be seen
Creator's gifts are expressed

&****&

Paws of Love
Part 2

All my married life; I have had a fine pet.
They help you with stress by making you forget.
Two guinea pigs; I had in the beginning.
I would watch them play, and was always grinning.

&****&

Then we received angora kitten as gift.
Watching her play around the house was a lift.
She was very pretty, white and a soft grey.
She would make us happy on any dark bleak day.

&****&

Then we had dogs; hunting dogs were only choice.
We had many good times, and we did rejoice.
An Irish setter was our first, called Sherry.
Hank would hunt her, and they came home quite merry.

&***&

Kitty paws gently flex with love on my chest.
My cats still do that; I found that is the best.
I remember times the dogs left wet paw prints.
That was better than when Josh had to wear splints.

&****&

Little paws or big; it doesn't matter size.
They were precious to me; this I must advise.
Paws of love are from pets you did own.
If you love a pet; you will not feel alone.

&****&

Christina's Choices

Christina is my name given at birth.
I write of nature and show you God's worth.
I try to write messages in my muse.
I write in a way that will not confuse.

&****&

My poetry is meant to uplift you.
Tranquility I bring you that is true.
My words come to your from angels of God.
They keep me on path of light that I trod.

&****&

Words come easily as they're from my core.
I hope many will read and will adore.
First five letters shows Jesus is within.
I was awoken to keep you from sin.

&****&

Angels are among us so stay on path.
Try to hold your temper and keep down wrath.

&****&

Living in God's Image

Faith
Is precious
Everyone does need
Faith increases through prayer
Times

&****&

Trust
Creator
Who made entire world
He made the mountains and great
Seas

&****&

Have
Loyalty
In Christian beliefs
Live in God's image each new
Day

&****&

Love
All people
Do not prejudice
Respect and honor all your
Meet

&***&

Pray
For all souls
That they rise above
Learn to forgive all who have
Hurt

&****&

Jesus Speaks

See,
All the birds
that fly so high.
I created for you.
Watching them will bring you great peace.
They fear not because they have trust in me.
They enjoy each day providing for all their young.
You must have faith like all the animals.
They know they'll find food and shelter.
Hard times they use feeders.
They feel refreshed
When springtime
comes.

&****&

Feel,
Like rebirth
in spring season.
Set time aside to pray.
Talk to me and tell me problems.
I will listen and bring you comfort.
Try to live in my image and you will succeed.
All will then see my spirit within you.
Your face will then have a great glow.
Challenges you will meet.
Many will then
Accept me
Too.

&****&

Effects of Spiritual Waters

Spiritual water we all need.
We try to do others good deed.
It helps us with those we should heed.

&****&

We will not thirst with this inside.
A Christian glow we can not hide.
All Commandments we will abide.

&****&

Our faith will grow in great measure.
Our God we consider treasure.
Our blessed love will bring us pleasure.

&****&

Our outlook on life is better.
When it's cool, we wear a sweater.
We enjoy things done together.

&****&

In a storm we can remain calm.
We sense things before and alarm.
We know when to beware of charm.

&****&

Spiritual essence we can share.
We can show others that we care.
We do not react with a dare.

&****&

For all Lonely People

God
Please give
The lonely
Wellness feeling
Show them light that helps to bring spirit up

&****&

Let them feel your arms surround them with love
Give them some hope
May they feel
Sorrows
Ease

&****&

Let
Their eyes
See your gifts
All around them
The glorious sunrise gives warmth to our homes

&****&

Sunset brings closure to a day well spent
Spend time wisely
What you do
Rewards
You

&****&

Just
Believe
In yourself
Accomplish goal
If at first you fail; do try it again

&****&

Relativity of Time

**Timeless,
are our treasures.
They're love we hold in our heart.
It's our commitment to Jesus.
They are always with us**

&**&**

**Respect,
all time given.
Use each hour the best you can.
Be thankful for all your free time.
Praise Jesus when you can.**

&**&**

**Honor,
all hard workers.
They use skills that God did give.
They live and use their time wisely.
They show pride in their work.**

&**&**

**Reflect,
on memories.
Be thankful you had these times.
Live in the image of Jesus.
You will be respected.**

&**&**

Forgiveness

**Forgiveness,
is good thing.
Peace it will then bring.
It lets you begin things anew.
There will be less days when you feel blue.
It will be like opening up new page.
You might splurge buying latest rage.
You will have more energy.
Thoughts will be better,
Adapting to
a new life.**

&*&**

**You can deal,
with much ease.
You'll know how to please.
You will look forward to each morn.
You will make plans beginning of dawn.
Your heart no longer burdened, you'll feel good.
You'll attempt goals knowing you could.
You'll be a better person.
Your great example,
by loving
everyone.**

&**&**

Wildflower Meadows

Wildflowers meadows are precious
Birds, bees, and butterflies visit
The gentle breeze blows the fragrance
Small birds hide among the tall stems
The view is an artist's pallet
Scene is vision of God's glory

&****&

Tranquility is felt by all
Birds might rest on the blossoms too
Bunnies scurry among flowers
Kitties hunt among the tall grass
The mountains are in the background
Wildflower meadows are precious

&****&

A brook runs along flower bed
Deer and small mammals quench their thirst
There are fresh water fish here too
Sometimes men fly fish from the brook
Sometimes families picnic here
Birds, bees, and butterflies visit

&****&

A young couple picks a bouquet
Girl wears the flower in her hair
They walk around watching nature
They watch a hawk flying over
She spots a hare in the willows
The gentle breeze blows the fragrance

&****&

The brook is busy place at dusk
Wildlife meets to enjoy a drink
Mosquitoes and fireflies are seen
Children try to catch lightning bugs
Birds chatter as darkness come in
Small birds hide among the tall stems

&****&

Colors of flowers are vibrant
They blend in showing many kinds
Birds carry seeds multiplying
The rain brings worms to surface
Birds hopping around enjoy meal
The view is an artist's pallet

&****&

Mountains near offer a great climb
There are hiking trails to follow
Endangered species protected
Scenic spot for relaxation
Nature walks are available
Scene is vision of God's glory

&****&

The Good Neighbor

Rose checks on elderly neighbor each day
Martha looks forward to her friendly care
Rose looks out for her as the Christian way
Martha drinks tea as her life she does share
Rose sees widow's hardships and is aware
Rose is alone but has family near
Martha's children are far, bringing a tear

&****&

Rose knows that she misses them a great deal
Whenever she speaks of them, her face glows
She talks of them showing how she does feel
Rose sees her love, from her head to her toes
Happiness she expresses as love flows
Rose's comfort keeps her from being sad
Rose knows she appreciates and is glad

&****&

Each woman does have need of the other
Rose feels great when she has left Martha's place
They share their friendship, but do not smother
She left her with a big smile on her face
They'll hold these memories and not erase
The companionship they share they both need
Rose feels wonderful doing this great deed.

&****&

Rose treats all like she wants to be treated
Rose practices commandments of God
Her good deeds she has always repeated
She walks the path of light in any sod
She's confident she does will of our Lord
Our role in life should always show the good
Do unto others like you know you should

&****&

- This is inspired fiction

The Promised Land

The Promised Land awaits all of us
Live life your best and in God trust
Do try to make wise choices
Hear the angel's voices
Let vision be clear
God please be near
Hear my plea
Set me
Free

&****&

Comfort
My family
Help them to deal with this
Dry their tears and help them to heal
Let memories we shared comfort them now
Help their healing to begin soon
I'll be with them always
Let them know this
Comfort

&****&

I feel presence Lord
I am ascending stairway
My soul is released

&****&

Angels do greet me
I see many that I know
We share warm embrace

&****&

Memories linger
They are tucked within my soul
Peace I now send them

&****&

The Peacemakers

Blessed be peacemakers that walk the earth.
They always have uplifting things to say.
They have a way to lift sorrow with mirth.
They smile at all throughout the toughest day.

&****&

Their optimistic viewpoint is the best.
They appreciate the little things too.
They help others with fears so they can rest.
They will keep away depression from you.

&****&

Their way of looking at life is better.
Spirit guides them to help all that they can.
Their friends learn to cope and not be fretter.
They'll spend time with you so you'll understand.

&****&

They teach forgiveness to all that they meet.
They build up their friendships with valued trust.
Once the slate is wiped clean, they won't repeat.
Those friendships are genuine and a must.

&****&

Value all the relationships you make.
Handle them with truth and never forsake.

&****&

*Extended Sonnet. I have one extra quatrain within this one.

God Speaks Through me

Father, I love thee
I try to show fulfillment
I praise you each day
Mold me to your requirement
You give my inspiration

&****&

Child, I see attempt
Others will realize this
You write as you are told
Go now and do not worry
Their sight will be opened now

&****&

Poetry

Poetry
is writing with soul.
We process
memories.
Sometimes we begin subject.
It gives us pleasure.

&****&

Spirit guides,
giving messages.
We listen,
and process
all into creative muse.
We then feel alive.

&****&

God's Creation

The awesome bright stars
Behold breathtaking waters
Turquoise possibilities
The peaceful mountains behind
Beautiful countryside charm

&****&

Turquoise frothy waves
Aqua-marine blue
Glistening lifting motion
Mighty Atlantic ocean
Restless majestic sound

&****&

Philosophy of Life
(ABC Senryu)

Appreciate all
Blessed gifts surround beauty
Creator did well

&****&

Desire for peace too
Each of us needs to accept
First you must repent

&****&

Greet all with kindness
Help another that's in need
In faith use patience

&****&

Judge no other soul
Kingdom of Heaven does that
Let justice prevail

&****&

Make friends to lonely
No one likes to be alone
Often pray to God

&***&

Prepare with wisdom
Quarreling does not solve things
Realize all good

&****&

Seek Christ in your heart
Trust spirit you have inside
Under stress seek help

&****&

Value your friendships
Warm friendships last forever
X-ray carefully

&****&

Yield for happiness
Zigzag if stops are needed
That's your A B C.

&****&

Guardian Angels

Angels from Heaven are here
They are sent to embrace us when we have fear
They calm a frightened small child
They keep us from danger when the winds are wild
Visits may be sequential
They're within business and residential
It's not coincidental

&****&

They will do bidding of God
You might meet one on path of light you do trod
They will do the assigned task
They may be answer to prayer that you did ask
They will return to Heaven
They may do his will on special day seven
They do help bread to leaven

&****&

A Week in Time

There are seven days in week
In each of these days it is God we should seek
His blessings surround us too
See his sunrise you found delightful to view
He offers eternal peace
He accepts everyone when their sins to cease
Heaven he gives as release

&****&

*Seventh Heaven—This form was created by Joseph Spence Sr.
© 10/21/2007 All rights reserved

My Christmas Wish

My Christmas wish is that all accept God.
All today accept his invitation.
Let us all join walking path of light trod.
You will then praise him with admiration.

&****&

Essence of your heart will be great story.
Holy Spirit will flow through you with ease.
All that you endure will then find glory.
Harsh words said of you will no longer tease.

&****&

Whenever you stumble he will pick up.
All trials you will feel his assistance too.
You will offer others spiritual cup.
You will feel him walking there beside you.

&****&

You will hear holy angels singing sweet.
His messages inside of you repeat.

&****&

God's Blessings

God gives us sunshine
The birds sing us melodies
Sun lifts our spirit

&****&

The bright sun will glow
Daylight brings warmth for us all
Cats will nap a lot

&****&

Bluejays notes are sweet
Small buds start to sprout on trees
Crocuses do bloom

&****&

The birds start bathing
Birdfeeders we then fill up
Gardens are alive

&****&

Moon phases are viewed
Stars glitter in the night sky
Comets might fly by

&****&

Ice on mountains melt
Brooks and streams are refilled too
Spring has now begun

&****&

This Poet's Reflection

Poets find peace in rereading their work.
They are at peace with themselves when they write.
It uplifts them giving them needed perk.
They are happy when other's find delight.

&****&

The essence of my soul then comes alive.
My purpose is to write to uplift you.
I'll write the best way I find to survive.
These words I write from my heart are quite true.

&****&

If memory is lost, I'll be just fine.
I'll refresh myself by reading once more.
Cherishing events I wrote like fine wine.
Poetry has opened up finest door.

&****&

My skill and subject come from divine Lord.
May he bless you all on path that you trod!

&****&

Valentines Day

Valentines Day is a day to show that you care
Always send out cards made with love to share
Love needs replenishment, not just once a year
Essential to express your love to all that are dear
Notes of love in a lunch can bring joy to your man
Tender sharing moments with compassion understand
In all you do; show the love you feel
Never hold a grudge; learn how to daily deal
Eager to commit; be sure that your love is real
Sincere love is accomplished with a blessing from God

&****&

Daily thanks for all your bounty from our Lord
Accept the things that you know you can't change
Yearn for the things you can mold and rearrange

&****&

Christmas Season
Two Word Acrostic

Appreciate beauty
Believe Christ
Creates dreams
Desire eternal
Everlasting future
Forever grateful
Giving hope
Hope illustrated
In Jesus
Jesus King
King lets
Learn mistakes
Mothers need
Never oppose
Omnipotent priorities
Priorities quiver
Quest recalling
Realization Savior
Savior truly
Teaches understanding
Using vital
Valuable words
With Xmas
Xylophone yielding
Yodeling zestfulness
Zeal appreciated

&*****&

Angelic Intervention

Fluttering away on angel's wings
My guardian angel help brings
He took me from burning car
He placed not very far
Rescuers then find
It blew their mind
I escaped
Burning
Car

&****&

There
Witness
Saw a man
He did carry
Me from burning car
Guardian was my Dad
I felt his love and was glad
He had left us as he was ill
His promise he would always fulfill

&****&

Know they're angels here
You'll never know when appear
They help us with fear

&****&

Spiritual Healers

Spiritual healers are gifts from God.
You may brush up against one on the street.
They know each day is blessing from our Lord.
Their praise for God they will often repeat.

&****&

Their words sometimes can help someone that's sick.
Their faith does persevere when all else fails.
Healing hands that touch are never a trick.
The essence of their heart has fullest sails.

&****&

They are beautiful both inside and out.
I hope my words can comfort all that read.
They pray to God when they have any doubt.
May my poetry flourish like a seed.

&****&

Healing with words is how I try to write.
May each poem read bring you great delight.

&****&

Healing with hands is not my gift.
I bring peace as your mind does drift.
Read my essence and feel my heart.
Now I hope I've given you jump-start.

&****&

ABC Two Word Acrostic

Always cheer
Bringing delight

&***&

Crave eternal
Deciding future

&****&

Eternally grateful
For Heaven

&****&

God Intervenes,
His judgment
Illustrates Kingly

&****&

Jesus lives
Kingly Majestic

&***&

Learn now
Many offerings

&***&

Needed patience
On quest
Providing realistic
Quorums stating
Real trust

&*&**

Savior understands
True value

&**&**

Undo world
Vision's x-ray
With yesterdays
Xv zenith

&*&**

Yes always
Zero bedevil!

&**&**

*****I have grouped this way to show you the thought process. This was a challenge I issued on a two word acrostic.**

The Ark

The ark was filled from sill to sill
with many animals.
They were bedded down
closely in harmony.
They were creatures from our God's treasury.
They were well cared for in the close quarters.
They would endure trip and would find peace.
In this new world wars would all cease.
A dove was sent out to see if it found land.
It returned tired not wanting to even stand.
Again returning, but he brought back a twig.
Noah's family would celebrate dancing a jig.
Noah knew now that land was certainly very near.
He had always remained confident and had no fear.
Soon the animals would be unloaded at their new home.
All pairs would start their own breed
never ever being alone.
They had all seen floodwaters, and they wished to
never ever see this thing again.
God sent a rainbow showing them that they must
remember what had happened then.
Now they would begin lives with faith, trust and love
in the Creator and Almighty God.
Remember the rainbow as sign from God and always
walk the path of light that Jesus trod.

&****&

The Golden Rule

"Do unto others as you want to be treated."
These words given by angels often repeated.
I know in my heart I treat all with required peace.
It would help when triggers that annoy do cease.

&****&

Examine your heart and realize will of God.
Now, you may walk the path of light that you have trod.
I harbor no ill will to those that caused me harm.
I do want to say that their actions caused alarm.

&****&

My heart and faith I will share with all that do read.
Spirit guides message now so that it will succeed.
Father, help all that need this message to read this.
This rule should apply to each day giving us bliss.

&****&

If all would apply this, our world would be just great.
All would live in harmony and appreciate.
Let all that have forgotten this start to now use.
Your life will be happier never lighting fuse.

&****&

My Rainbow

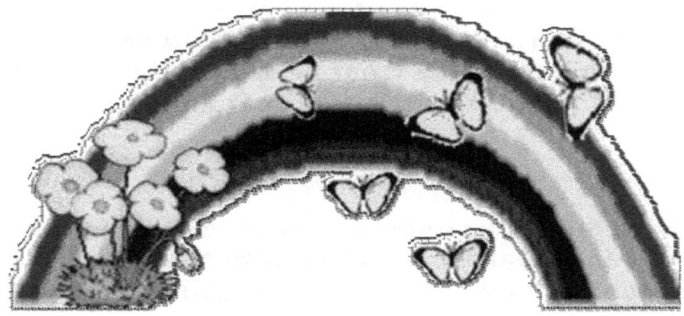

My rainbow had five streams of only red.
Each stream represents day of the week.
I thought about this when I went to bed.
Now I believe I will get peace I seek.

&****&

The color red stands for blood God did shed
I have given troubles over to him.
This analysis came into my head.
Now I feel that my future's not so dim.

&****&

I will go to work now forgetting all.
My mind will just concentrate on each task.
In the eyes of God I do feel quite tall.
He knows what I need, I don't have to ask.

&****&

I'll remember this rainbow forever.
God's beside me in all types of weather.

&****&

Thunder in the Heavens

Have no fear, angels are clapping their hands.
The thunder can do no damage at all.
God's glory's seen with vivid lightning bands.
There may be some dead branches that may fall.

&****&

My Mom would tell me this to stop my fear.
The lightning to me is anger of God.
When I hear thunder now, I feel she's near.
Please beware of the path that you do trod.

&****&

Someday heavens will open in glory.
Trumpets will blast and angels will be heard.
God will call up cherished as in story.
This is what is written as is God's word.

&****&

Graves will open and families will rise.
Be among the blessed as this is quite wise.

&****&

Heaven on Earth

Heaven I feel when I write poetry.
Advice to you I bring from inner core.
Messages I bring for the world to see.
Important is God is forevermore.

&****&

I feel Heaven when with my family.
Shopping with my Daughter brings me pleasure.
Family is assets of treasury.
Time spent together is beyond measure.

&****&

Heaven's felt when I see sun rise and set.
The bird's playing a melody is great.
These are God's creations, please don't forget.
This is something I do appreciate.

&****&

Cherished things are friendship and also love.
This is given to us from God above.

Perseverance

Perseverance we all do need

Each day do ask God to succeed

Realize that God is the light

Sincere gratitude gives insight

Every time you stumble he's there

Very aware God shows he does care

Each day be thankful for our God

Remember gifts given by our Lord

Also when defeated you still ate

Never do fail to appreciate

Call on him when things are dim

Enjoy moments given by him

&****&

Prayer for Reduction of Stress

God do help those that do have strife
Please help them to go on with life
All their dealings are sharp as knife

&****&

They are in this horrid pattern, where all is going wrong
It seems the harder they do try, something does not belong
Please aid all those individuals and help them be real strong

&****&

They need your help very much
They are awaiting your touch
They feel like their going Dutch

&****&

They need to feel calm
Now they feel alarm
They need lucky charm

&***&

I place faith in you
I know you'll come through
They will not feel blue

&****&

Prayer for Asthmatics

God help those that now do suffer
Let lungs begin to get tougher
Help climate to not get rougher

&***&

Some of us have both inside and outside allergies too
Breathing does become chore in everything we try to do
Father ease trauma we go through daily, and I thank you

&***&

With my faith; I remain strong
God heard and will not be long
I must praise in Bible song

&****&

His presence does calm
I don't feel alarm
He is lucky charm

&****&

I feel his being
I wish was seeing
Danger now fleeing

&****&

Crisp Autumn Air

Air crispness,
is not felt
The air feels fresh and really quite clean
Magnificent colors are seen very soon
My favorite is when the burning bush turns red
It is fantastic version that will turn all heads
Bright chrysanthemums bloom
Yards have many colors
Autumn is
quite pretty

&****&

Trees turn hues,
that makes news
New England is noted for its view
Tourists will travel to view the scene
The trees look spectacular with their autumn hat
Restaurants do well as there are more people out
Pumpkins kids have fun with
They decorate with face
Hay rides too,
You may see

&****&

Christmas Acrostics

Christmas is a time of happiness and sorrow
Hear the angels sing of promise of tomorrow
Realize that God offers us everlasting reward
In all you do; stop hating that cuts like a sword
Seek Jesus out and you will never feel bored
Teach children only in redemption you will win
Make a promise to try hard not to create a sin
Ask to be forgiven and you will be given a new life
Surely with God at your side you'll handle all strife

&****&

Christmas decorations and trees are bought
Hear that many shoplifters are being caught
Reindeer and sleds are lit up on people's lawn
Inspiration felt by many at early dawn
Santa's are seen in malls throughout the land
Trendy things bought and kids feel all's grand
Mother's make cookies and pies with great love
Always take time to thank God from above
Send somebody peace offering with a dove

&****&

Christmas carolers join to sing at someone's house
Hardly a noise upstairs as kids are quiet as mouse
Reindeer hoofs are heard going clip clop, clip clop
In most cases a screech is heard when they stop
Santa is heard belching as he eats his cookie snack
Tired after long night, Santa begins to rub his back
"Merry Christmas Ho, Ho, Ho," is what Santa said
Always a child hears and then will go back to bed
Santa climbs up the chimney back up to his sled

&****&

Happy New Year

Have a healthy year
Hope your memories are dear
Hear the angels sing

&****&

Appreciate all
Acclaim merits you did earn
Atone for all sins

&****&

Pray to God each day
Patiently use time wisely
Plan to do better

&****&

Praise God in your acts
Prepare your meals healthily
Plan to learn new things

&***&

Yearn for Heaven's peace
Yield in bad situations
Yank from devils hold

&****&

Nag no one ever
Negotiate all contracts
Never lose your faith

&****&

Express all you feel
Each day try to help someone
Examine conscience

&****&

Weigh good and the bad
Walk on the path of the light
Welcome new friendships

&****&

Yell hardly ever
Yodel only in contest
Yawn when are alone

&***&

Earn what you work for
Exert effort in all things
Edit all you write

&****&

Accept God in life
Account to him in all you do
Admire all good things

&****&

Reach for stars above
Radiate God's love within
Recline for some rest

&****&

*This was a triple Acrostic challenge I created

God's Advice to all

Appreciate beautiful creatures

Destiny eternal fulfillment

God's holiness illustrated

Kaleidoscope leaves memories

Nurses often pressured

Quit real sins

Teach universal values

Win x-rays yielding zest

&****&

**This picture is on the cover of my book
Amazing Pets & Animals**

Kodak Moment

Child building sand castles in sand
Stepping on pebbles on the shore
Collecting seashells for project
A child watching fireworks first time
Your child's first steps learning to walk
Riding two wheel bike without fall

&****&

Standing on boardwalk watching all
Playing volleyball in the sand
Realizing that you can float well
Child losing bathing suit at beach
Expression when bit by a crab
Child building sand castles in sand

&****&

Floating for the very first time
Getting baked in the sun for tan
Burying their Dad in the sand
Child's first attempt at dodging cars
Child's face when on rollercoaster
Stepping on pebbles on the shore

&****&

Child crawling backwards on their back
Your child's first words and what they were
First day of school and taking bus
Your child's sweetheart at their school
Attending their very first dance
Collecting seashells for project

&****&

Their first trip to amusement park
Eating cotton candy at fair
Their first ride on carousel horse
Riding Ferris wheel up so high
Riding the small train with their Mom
A Child watching fireworks for first time

&***&

Their first haircut and expression
Closing their mouth for the Dentist
Getting their first pair of earrings
Seeing their gifts on first Christmas
Collecting treats Easter morning
Your child's first steps learning to walk

&****&

Playing on their own gym in yard
Sliding down the slide into dirt
Learning how to rollerblade well
Attempting to ice skate at park
Playing girls soccer in springtime
Riding two wheel bike without fall

&****&

My Feelings on my Death

I will feel joy and some grief on my demise.
I will hope that I did live my life quite wise.
I certainly will be quite happy above.
I will join all of my family I love.

&****&

We will have a great reunion then.
Face to face I'll speak to God time and again.
I will thank him for times he watched over me.
I will feel a great peace in his company.

&****&

I will feel sorrow for ones I left behind.
I will show them I am with them with a sign.
I will be sure they all feel my presence too.
They will know I am with them when they are blue.

&****&

I hope they will continue their lives with God.
Their strength will become stronger with our dear Lord.
Keep God first in your life to avoid all strife.
My love will be with you in all of your life.

&****&

Prayer for Retirees

God help those on pensions survive
Help them so they can stay alive
Keep them warm and spirit revive

&****&

The rich get richer and have more unnecessary greed
Middle class and poor are always the ones that are in need
Wicked get stronger and need to flourish like nasty weed
&****&

Share your faith with those without
Take away all of their doubt
Halleluiah, they shout!

&***&

I pray you hear plea
Hope you answer me
I do respect thee

&****&

Rents are out of sight
This can cause a fright
Faith must have great might

&****&

Life

Life is a blessing from our God
Life is path of light that I trod
Life is always great beginning
Life is ecstatic when winning

&****&

Life is helping someone you know
Life is seeing their face does glow
Life is giving friendship to all
Life is praising God as my call

&****&

Life is living each day as last
Life is letting go of all past
Life is to forgive those that harm
Life is to bring about with charm

&****&

Life is unconditional love
Life is a treasure from above
Life is vessel of emotions
Life is the best of all potions

&****&

Life is like a bowl of Jell-O
Life is vivid or quite mellow
Life is a shake that's up and down
Life is challenge God turns around

&****&

Life is beauty beyond measure
Life is family and pleasure
Life is what you choose it to be
Life is expressing poetry

&****&

The Aquatic Plants

Plants have importance
They have to keep water clean
They look really nice

&****&

Lilies are useful
Fish spawn on the lily pads
They benefit all

&****&

Plants keep algae down
Fish will remain quite healthy
They are important

&****&

هششۿششم

Weeds are different
They are not worthwhile at all
They should be removed

&****&

Weeds overtake pond
Fish here should not be eaten
Pond does pollute them

&****&

Ponds should be kept clean
No litter should be thrown in
This is quite vital

&****&

Keep fresh water clean
Do not use boat with motor
Oil pollutes the pond

&****&

Chariots of Fire

Chariots of fire are not what you may think.
It may be poem that stops abuse of drink.
I take you down the paths of memory too.
I try to keep poets from becoming blue.

&****&

The subjects I choose; I was inspired to write.
Most have something in there of our God's insight.
The words flow out faster than I can write down.
I hope to replace smile where face had a frown.

&****&

God is my mentor, and inspires me to write.
I hope my ramblings bring much delight.
I wake up in middle of night to write down.
Maybe one reads and their life will turn around.

&****&

Nature and all its beauty; I see each day.
I like to share this with you in my own way.
The fire felt is my passion, and soul I share.
Tips and knowledge; I now offer as I care.

&****&

I will pass down my poetry to others.
Right now I share with my sisters and brothers.
God gives me the beauty each day of my life.
May my work eliminate all of your strife.

&****&

Locks of Love

Each year some women cut their hair to give.
Their hair will make wig for sick child to live.
With cancer treatments most do lose some hair.
These women show their love and how they care.

&****&

It gives the children a feeling of joy.
It doesn't matter if they're a girl or boy.
All will appreciate the efforts made.
Their thankfulness will never ever fade.

&****&

Some donors have given more than once too.
They let it grow then cut with love so true.
They know their hair will bring someone a smile.
They will remember that for a long while.

&****&

Lock's of Loves organization is great.
All that benefit does appreciate.
They are caring and help those most in need.
Their talents are used in doing good deed.

&****&

It's great that places like this still exist.
It helps to fulfill the children's wish list.
I commend those that help achieve this goal.
They are showing a real true Christian soul.

&****&

Open Invitation of God

God invites us all to love him
With him beside you things aren't dim
Do not let him be just a whim

&****&

Know that he is real, and you can feel his spirit within
With his spirit within; you will try to avoid all sin
Accept Jesus in your prayer, and you will always win

&****&

With Jesus; life is better
He warms you like a sweater
Stand tall like field of heather

&****&

His beauty I see
It does surround me
See the tiny bee

&****&

Pollinates each bloom
Without would be doom
Flower scent in room

&****&

Morning Beginnings

The sun rises early this day
I hear birds chattering from trees
A cat waits to go in the house

&****&

Hummingbird sips the nectar drink
A hawk flies landing in large pine
The sun rises early this day

&****&

Mockingbird sings a loud chorus
Starlings hear and fly to feeder
I hear birds chattering from trees

&****&

Robins on grass eat juicy worms
Chipmunk scurries across the yard
A cat waits to go in the house

&****&

The Lilac

If I were a flower, a lilac I would be.
All would come by to sniff fragrance I had left thee.
It would be delight for hummingbirds and the bees.
Birds would rest in my branches feeling quite carefree

&****&

For at least a month, my fragrant blooms bring delight
The view from afar is a very pretty sight.
Hummingbirds would rest on my blossoms from long flight.
I can bloom on a shrub, or a tree that has height.

&****&

Deer would stay away as scent just enjoyed by man.
When my blooms die, butterfly bush is God's next plan.
My blooms can be cut for a bouquet, they can.
Petals would be great in potpourri dish with fan.

&****&

Enjoy my fragrance as it lingers in the air.
I take just a little fertilizer and care.
My fragrance may be a little strong, be aware.
Often my beauty I feel is beyond compare.

&****&

Lilacs give a scent that is sweet
In most zones they are grown quite neat
Lavender scent that you recall
A pretty focal point for all
Care and fertilizer make tall

&****&

My Soul's Flight

Essence of soul fly
Write the reason why
Vision do behold
Better than gold
Angels do greet
God we meet
Forgive
Me God
For Sins
And
Hear
Me
Now
As
Sad
And
Let my enter your kingdom

&****&

Chariots of Fire Part 2

This chariot of fire is not the one you know.
Here the fire I do light is the light of God's glow.
My brain records the beauty he has given us.
I then try to show you this beauty as I trust.

&****&

I can only say; I feel like a camcorder.
This beauty I then do write out like recorder.
Wildlife and nature are the things I love the most.
I only once did write of event with a ghost.

&****&

I hope my poetry show the path I am on.
I know poems will be passed down after I'm gone.
I always try to bring smiles to every face.
I want to be known as a fine lady with grace.

&****&

My Granddaughter loves poems with animal's best.
She asks to write about new animal as test.
She is eight this month and precious gem of my life.
When I am with her; I forget all of my strife.

&****&

With God in my corner; I will try to write well.
I believe he gives me good subjects which I tell.
When you visit, you do not need a library card.
What I write is easy to understand, not hard.

&****&

God's Blessings

God gives us sunshine
The birds sing us melodies
Sun lifts our spirit

&****&

The bright sun will glow
Daylight brings warmth for us all
Cats will nap a lot

&****&

Bluejay notes are sweet
Birdfeeders we then fill up
Gardens are alive

&****&

Moon phases are viewed
Stars glitter in the night sky
Comets might fly by

&****&

Ice on mountains melt
Brooks and streams are refilled too
Spring has now begun

&****&

The Invitation

Daily we have choices that we do make.
I want to tell you that God is not a fake.
Let him walk beside you every day.
Accept Jesus within your heart today.

&****&

You will gain strength as your faith will then grow.
People will see you're Christian and know.
You'll praise his Holy name in a great way.
Accept Jesus within your heart today.

&****&

He accepts all that want repentance too.
He is awaiting decision by you.
I am honored with words he gives to say.
Accept Jesus within your heart today.

&****&

He gave us freedom to make all choices.
Once you accept, you'll hear angel voices.

&****&

Angel Kisses

Angel kiss,
Is just bliss
As you feel their vibrations near you
You know that their love for you is true
They are with you when you are worried about things
All worries have been dealt with and now your heart sings
Your rest tonight is great
You do appreciate
Guardians
That protect

&****&

Protection,
Rejection
From any evil that we might face
They give us love and help us with grace
They distinguish the sheep that might be disguise
They help us with making decisions that are wise
They comfort when we're sad
They are with us when glad
They are our
Guardians

&****&

The Poet and the Artist

The poet and the artist were a team.
The portrait brought verse as the words did flow.
Artist painted a view of a moonbeam.
Vision on both their faces was a glow.

&****&

With the moon's beam, romance had filled the air.
The beauty of horizon had been shown.
Viewing heavens, the stars glistened with glare.
Peace was felt, as many angels had known.

&****&

The artist continued painting with heart.
The essence of her soul could then be seen.
She had only wished younger she did start.
She'd added crystal clear brook so pristine.

&****&

Be unique in the gift that God did give.
Let inspiration be with you to live.

&****&

*Inspired by a co-worker

The Blessed Trinity

In three ways the Blessed Trinity speaks of God.
Some do not understand this and find this quite odd.
All true Christians believe God is all of these things.
They know at entrance of heaven an angel sings.

&****&

Holy Spirit you do feel when accepting him.
Spirit helps you be calm when things grow quite dim.
You must pray for help and guidance when there's a need.
A small bit of faith will grow like a mustard seed.

&****&

God sent his Son for the redemption of all sin.
All that ask his forgiveness in the end will win.
Christians receive Holy Spirit when they're reborn.
Baptism offers this and then they're not forlorn.

&****&

Therefore God is the Father, Son, and Holy Ghost.
Jesus offers himself to all from coast to coast.
Be a believer and follower as I am.
Believe this shepherd takes care of all of his lamb.

&****&

My Vision

God release souls between heaven and hell.
I have seen vision that was warning bell.
A vision I once saw just came to me.
Please help them, as your love they want to see.

&****&

They are sorry that they did not forgive.
They really do want to in Heaven live.
I pray you release souls and give them flight.
Their families await them with delight.

&****&

Soul I saw was precious Aunt that I love.
She reckoned me to go back from above.
I had been in tunnel and I went through.
"Its not time, go back is what you must do."

&****&

I awoke to cat meowing near me.
Breathing was shallow and that he did see.
I had been in tunnel and I saw light.
I felt peace as I went through and great light.

&****&

Chronic asthma had been out of control.
I restored with treatment and then felt whole.
To enter Heaven, you must all forgive.
Bring Jesus in your heart and then you'll live.

&****&

Chariots of Fire Part 3

My chariot of fire is the soul of my muse.
I try to help those that are just a bit confused.
I write of experiences I have had too.
Many have God within, and I show this to you.

&****&

My poems are brought out by beauty I do see.
Sometimes it's just woodpecker eating from the ground.
Other times; I may see a squirrel act or two.
Even yet a chipmunk might appear in my view.

&****&

I find glory in all that God has given us.
I pray to him each day and I do place my trust.
I feel my spirits rise as I finish my work.
I just hope it is not reviewed by some real jerk.

&****&

The workshop lets you create and share all you are.
If you read enough; your talent will go quite far.
You do get inspired when you read someone else's too.
It sparks something and then the fire begins to brew.

&****&

I hope the various things I write you will like.
If not; just go read another or take a hike!
Humor is something I do also, as you see.
Laughter brings blood pressure down and that's good for thee.

&****&

Light of the World

I view the night stars
I then do see Mars
Big dipper I see
Pleasure to me
Brilliant light
Stairway flight
Angels
Singing
Chorus
Harps
Heard
Horns
Blast
Souls
Free
Rise
Speed to the gates of Heaven

&****&

The Timetable of God

Destiny is God's plan for you.
Keep him in your heart and be true.
Walking with God you'll find delight.
He answers needs when time is right.

&****&

Sometimes there may be fork in road.
Our troubles may be heavy load.
Keep praying and you'll find insight.
He answers needs when time is right.

&****&

A Sign he'll send for you to see.
Follow and know he is with thee.
He is with you on darkest night.
He answers needs when time is right.

&****&
God's plan becomes your destiny.
He answers needs when time is right.

&****&

Eternal Life Promised

God does give us eternal life
He does help us with all our strife
When we obey, we're better wife

&****&

He suffered greatly and died on a cross made from dogwood
His death had fulfilled prophesy as they said it should
The Dogwood tree from then on had trunk that had crooked wood

&****&

Shed his blood for all of us
It is in him we must trust
Pray to him daily is must

&****&

Repent sins to him
Future not so dim
He is not a whim

&****&

Walk the path of light
He will bring delight
Heaven's in your sight

&****&

A Day I'll Treasure

I walked into the kitchen in great awe.
The entire kitchen had a reddish glow.
A rainbow band of five arches I saw.
I stepped out to realize; why was so.

&****&

I went inside beginning to ponder.
Rainbow then just blended with sky all blue.
Eyes looked to East as rainbow was yonder.
All at once I realized and I knew.

&****&

We had been discussing some work issues.
God had heard of my plight and sent a sign.
Ongoing problems required some tissues.
I looked again and then saw his remind.

&****&

Rainbow bands had returned for me to see.
I then knew God was looking out for me.

&****&

Effects of Jealously

Jealously,
Makes all sad
That is why you're mad
Be glad and forget of the past
The mold was sculptured and did not last
Let us go on now the way that we should
Is it possible we both could?
Forgive the past and start new
That's the only way
To save our
Cherished love

&****&

Heartbreak does,
Heal with care
You must be aware
Healing must be slow and steady
Harboring those memories does no good
Things are now the way they should
God tells us all to forgive
This is only way
For you to
Be content

&****&

Mustard Seed of Faith

Seed of faith, begins very small
As faith increases, we feel tall
When we lose faith, we increase sins
Very small seed of faith begins

&****&

God does guide us, when we do pray
He helps keep temptation away
As faith increases, we then trust
When we do pray, God does guide us

&****&

Your faith you can show, when you write
Your poems will give some insight
You will know they enjoyed, and glow
When you write, your faith you can show

&****&

You will share your faith with others
You'll treat like sisters and brothers
You will all show that you do car
Your faith with others you will share

&****&

My Bright White Star

My star would be a beautiful bright white.
As I view it; it would bring me delight.
I would look at it and think of my dream.
I would hope that some day my star would gleam.

&****&

I would think about my goals in life.
I would try to live through all of the strife.
I would attempt what I set out to do.
I would ask for God's strength to pull me through.

&****&

ﻣششО̂شش

I am trying to write in many ways.
I enjoy new techniques learned on some days.
A new poetic form I do enjoy.
These new forms will bring me hours of great joy.

&****&

My poetry must not be all the same.
I write many styles almost like a game.
My subjects are varied as black and white.
I want to give my readers great delight.

&****&

I can write as myself or another.
I write many tributes to my Mother.
I try to keep my themes really upbeat.
I try not to ever write of defeat.

&****&

I choose bright white as the star of God's birth.
I really feel this color has great worth.
I will focus on my star on each day.
I think of it when I kneel down to pray.

&****&

My King
(Tina-Rhyme)

My King

Makes heart sing

You're the answer for all

You're there whenever we call

It is to you I pray and do seek

It is you I talk to every day of the week

My soul treasures messages that you may send.

It's up to you I hope to ascend

You help me throughout each day

It is the only way

You are there

And care

&****&

*This style was created by Chazz Combs. See Glossary for instructions.

Holy Spirit

Holy Spirit guides
It is from within
Essence is of God
Hear message he gives
Obey commandment

&****&

It's always there
We are aware
Trust what you're told
You'll feel fulfilled

&****&

It directs
You follow
Gratefully

&****&

Listen
Angel's

&****&

Harps

&****&

Jesus has Risen

Body rose on third day
He was seen leaving tomb
Stone removed on day three
His garments had been left
This was the prophecy

&****&

Body rose on third day
All that heard did rejoice
Halleluiah heard!
He would meet disciples
All did listen for word

&****&

Body rose on third day
Mary now felt some release
Her faith was very strong
This was what angel told
She now heard angel's song

&****&

Body rose on third day
He met with disciples
Advice Jesus now gave
Thomas saw the nail marks
He sent them out to save

&****&

Body rose on third day
On Easter we rejoice
Choirs and people do sing
His spirit we do feel
Words of God I now bring

&****&

Hopes and Dreams
*Italian Sonnet

It is good to have dreams to hold on to
Glory is vision we see in our dreams
A goal we try to reach without extremes
People show respect when they look at you
Your life seems to have a different hue
When goal is reached it may not be as seams
Happiness may be shown in face that gleams
Keep your faith and keep doing what you do

&****&

Trust intuition in doing your best
Pray to restore faith in what you have done
Angels will guide you on your path in life
Spirit will guide you in doing the rest
Accept the outcome knowing you have won
Accomplishments do help you with all strife

&****&

Summer's Beauty

Sun raises high in the sky to warm us.
Fuchsia blooms of Rose of Sharon are seen.
We begin each day with "In God I trust."
The bird's water must be kept really clean.

&****&

Wildflowers stems sway gently in the breeze.
Hummingbirds fly back and forth from flowers.
Some are seen relaxing on porch with ease.
Soft wind accompanies gentle showers.

&****&

The cunning squirrel drinks the nectar brew.
Bees and hornets annoy the hummingbirds.
It did not take long to learn something new.
Melodies and chatter are heard from birds.

&****&

At dusk the deer will come to the feeder.
The Mother arrives first as the leader.

&****&

The Fall Portrait

Cotoneaster's changed
The leaves now have reddish hues
Later they lose leaves

&****&

These are good for nests
Birds will hide between branches
Leaves grow back in spring

&****&

**Holly has berries
These red berries adorn bush
They provide food too**

&****&

**Some trees lost all leaves
Colorful leaves carpet ground
Squirrels store some food**

&****&

**Some bushes turn red
Burning bush looks fantastic
There is nip in air**

&****&

**Nature prepares now
All know cold weather's ahead
Strong survive each breed**

&**&**

**God gives us seasons
All look forward to next spring
It is great rebirth**

&**&**

Tree Rings
(Haiku/Senryu)

Each ring is one year
Older trees will have wide trunk
They may live long time

&****&

Some hard woods are cut
This may be used for firewood
Oak is a hard wood

&***&

Some die through lightning
When struck they will crash down hard
Wood may heat a home

&****&

Others get diseased
Ants or termites might eat them
They become hollow

&****&

Sometimes a fire kills
This timber would be wasted
This is a real shame

&****&

God determines death
There should always be new growth
Grow with help of God

&****&

The Fireflies

Fireflies glow at night
They glow a yellow green light
They eat other bugs

&****&

They glow on and off
This is how they attract mate
Are called lightning bugs

&****&

They can be caught too
If caught; put them in a jar
Release in short time

&****&

They can't live in jar
They need to fly and be free
Carnivorous too

&****&

They eat each other
Watch out if others get close
They could be hungry

&****&

They are works of art
God created them for us
Appreciate them

&****&

هششهÔهششه

Envy
*Tetractys

We
Should not
Envy those
That do have more
We should focus on blessings we have

&****&

At some point we all envied another
We have the stars
That light the
Dark night
Sky

&***&

Then
The moon
Shines brightly
Bringing romance
The moon and the stars are beautiful to see

&****&

Then we have the precious sunrise each day
It brings us hope
Of pleasant
Warm new
Day

&***&

Then
At dusk
The sun sets
Gives awesome hue
The crimson auburn sunset is quite precious

&****&

If you watch the sunset you'll feel great peace
Brings renewal
And closure
To our
Day

&****&
These
Are
All
Blessings we
Have been given
Praise Almighty God for blessings he gives

&****&

My Muse (Choka)

My muse should be clear
Messages I try to give
Poetry is soul

&****&

Often spirit guides my quill
I cooperate
These messages have value

&****&

My soul's uplifted
I have followed Master's will
Listen to angels

&****&

Angels walk the earth with you
They may be disguised as friends

&****&

Essence (Monorhyme)

Essence of my soul helps me write
Encounters occurred caused some fright
Soul flow's freely bringing delight
Let me show a beautiful sight
Try very hard with all my might
Yes, read now letting soul take flight

&****&

Love Shared

Timeless,
Is love we have known
It remains a part of our heart
Memories,
We've shared are embedded there too
We enjoyed throughout our lives
Always

&****&

هششهٌششه

Forget,
Not those that have gone
Keep them in your heart forever
Realize,
They watch over every day
They're our guardian angels
Precious

&**&**

Recall,
All the times you shared
Their love you will now start to feel
Genuine,
Love and their spirit you will sense
Your sadness replaced with joy
Grateful

&**&**

Believing in Jesus

Father,
I try my best.
Help me to explain things.
I have never seen the nail marks,
Yet I know you suffered a lot for us.
We are all worthy of your love.
Give correct words to write.
Mold me like you,
Father.

&****&

Desire,
To give answers.
Help me to express well.
Some have needed your assistance.
I believe they needed to ask your help.
My feelings are they are afraid.
You would then bring comfort.
You're always my
Desire.

&****&

Forgive,
Them now Father.
They're unsure of approach.
Give me words of comprehension.
Let my words ring out to them loud and clear.
Let them then walk the path of light.
I will share your spirit.
Bless those that do
Forgive

&****&

Poetry Glossary Page 1

Acrostic Poetry

Acrostic Poetry is where the first letter of each line spells a word, usually using the same words as in the title.

ABC Darien

An ABC Darien poem is a poem creation where each successive word begins with the next letter in the alphabet until you have reached the letter Z.

Candlelight

Candlelight---Poetry form created by Christina R Jussaume on 12/03/07. Syllable counts are 5, 5, 5, 4, 4, 3, 2, 2, 2, 1, 1, 1, 1, 1, 1, 1 and 7 syllables.
RHYME is AABBCCDEFGHIJKLMN

Cascade

Cascade, a form created by Udit Bhatia, is all about receptiveness, but in smooth cascading way like a waterfall. The poem does not have any rhyme scheme; therefore, the layout is simple. Say the first verse has three lines. Line one of verse one becomes the last line of verse two. To follow suit, the second line of verse one becomes the last line of verse three. The third line of verse one now becomes the last line of verse four, the last stanza of the poem.

RHYME is a/b/c d/e/A, f/g/B, h/i/C

To make the Cascade an even longer poem, use more lines in verse one. For example, if verse one has six lines, the poem must have seven stanzas so that each line of verse one is reused as a refrain in each following stanza.

&****&

Poetry Glossary Page 2

Constanza

The Constanza, created by Connie Marcum Wong, consists of five or more 3 line stanzas. Each line has a set meter of eight syllables. The first lines of all the stanzas can be read successively as an independent poem, with the rest of the poem weaved in to express a deeper meaning. The first lines convey a theme written in monorhyme, while the second and third lines of each stanza rhyme together.

Rhyme scheme :   a b b, a c c, a d d, a e e, a f f etc.

Butterfly

This form was created by Michael Degenhardt. This has 9 lines starting with 5 syllables, rhyming not needed. Next line has 4, then 3, then 2, 2, 2, 3, 4, 5. Few words make better word choices.

Choka

Choka---A poem with a 575, 575, 575, 575, and 77 syllable count. There is no rhyme in this poem.

Christ-in-a-Rhyme

The Christ-in-a-Rhyme, a shape poem of the spiritual nature was created by Christina R Jussaume on October3, 2006. It consists of five 3 lined stanzas that must rhyme. Rhyme for this form is AAA BBB CCC DDD and EEE and a syllable count of each stanza is as follows.

Stanza 1---8 syllables	Stanza 2---14 syllables
Stanza 3—7 syllables	Stanza 4 and 5—5 syllables

The poem should be centered to show the cross that will be created. This form was created in memory of her Mother, Christina.

&****&

Poetry Glossary Page 3

Diatelle

The Diatelle is a fun, syllable counting form like the Etheree with a twist. The syllable structure of the Diatelle is as follows: /2/3/4/6/8/10/12/10/8/6/4/3/2/1, but unlike the Etheree, has a set rhyme pattern of Abbcbccaccbcbba. This poetry form may be written on any subject and looks best center aligned in a diamond shape. It was created by Bradley Vrooman.

Eight by Four (8 X 4) Syllable

8 x 4 Sentence: Eight lines of four syllables each. This results in one complete sentence! This form was created by Alvin Othto Stewart © 2007.

English Pensee

The English Cameo is an unrhymed poem done in the syllabic counts of 2 5 8 3 7 and 2.

French Rime Royal

This is a French form made popular by an Englishman Geoffrey Chaucer. It is named after a Scottish king-King James I; it has an Italian pattern in it a Sicilian triplet. It is iambic pentameter with a rhyme scheme of ababbcc
    dedeeff ghghhii etc. Each stanza is 9 lines and the number of stanzas is up to the poet

Poetry Glossary Page 4

Haiku

Most popular definition, but there is more to haiku than meets the eye. It is an unrhymed Japanese verse consisting of three lines of 5, 7, and 5 syllables. Haiku is usually written in the present tense and focuses on nature.

Jewels Rule

This form was created by Chazz Combs. It is a syllabic poem with a count of 4 7 7 4 4 7 7 4 4 7 7 and 4. Rhyme is aabbccddeeff

Joseph's Star

Joseph's Star—A poetry form created by Christina R Jussaume on 08 06 07 in memory of my Dad. This poem has no rhyme. It is written according to syllable counts. Syllables are 1, 3, 5, 7, 7, 5, 3, and 1. It should have complete statements in each line. It can be about any subject. It should be center aligned. There is no limit to the number of stanzas you can make.

Kyrielle Sonnet

A French form from middle ages. It has 14 lines..3 rhyming quatrains followed by a non-rhyming couplet. Each line has 8 syllables.
*Variations.. sometimes poets use this form with an ending rhyming couplet.

&****&

Poetry Glossary Page 5

Lucky Leaf

A Poetry form created by Christina R Jussaume on 08 22 07. The form should be center aligned to give the shape of clover. Syllables ar 3, 3, 9, 9, 12, 12, 6, 6, 3, and 3. It can be any subject with or without rhyme.

Michelle's Heart

A Poetry form created by Christina R Jussaume on 08 10 07. I created this shaped poetry form for my Daughter Michelle. It is a poem of 11 lines. Syllable count is 3 3 5 8 9 10 8 7 5 3 and 3. Subject is optional. It should be center aligned to show the shape of heart. Rhyme scheme is ABBCCDDEFGH

Monchielle

The Monchielle is a poem that consists of four five-ine stanzas where the first line repeats in each verse. Each line within the stanzas consists of six syllables, and lines three and five rhyme. The rhyme pattern is Abcdc Aefgf
Ahihi Aklml. The Monchielle form was created by Jim T. Henriksen.

Monorhyme

A Monorhyme is a poem in which all the lines have the same end rhyme.

&****&

Poetry Glossary Page 6

Monotetra

The Monotetra is a new poetic form developed by Michael Walker. Each stanza contains four lines in monorhyme. Each line is in tetrameter (four metrical feet) for a total of eight syllables. What makes the monotetra so powerful as a poetic form, is that the last line contains two metrical feet, repeated. The last line has a verse of 4 syllables repeated giving the total of 8 syllables for the line.

Line 1: 8 syllables A1
Line 2: 8 syllables A2
Line 3: 8 syllables A3
Line 4: 8 syllables, repeated; A4 A4.

Nonet

A Nonet has nine lines. The first line has nine syllables, the second line eight syllables, the third line seven syllables, etc.. until line nine that finishes with one syllable. It can be any subject matter and rhyme is optional. Created by Mark Williams © 2003

Pentaphor

A Pentaphor should be left aligned. It is a syllabic poem that is easy to do. First Stanza has five syllables, five lines, and then four syllables four lines, then three syllables three lines, two syllables and two lines and last one is one syllable, one last line. It is a five stanza poem without rhyme. It can be any subject.

&****&

Poetry Glossary Page 7

Patricia's Harmony

This form was created by Christina R Jussaume as a tribute to poet, Patricia Ann Farnsworth Simpson. The form starts with four Senyru. These Senyru begin with the letters P A T R I C I A S H A and R. Next 8 syllable count Quatrain in rhyme. This must start with the letters M O N Y. The poem must be spiritual in nature. I have incorporated an Acrostic, Senyru and Quatrain style within this creation of mine.

Quatrain

A Quatrain is a poem consisting of four lines of verse with a specific rhyming scheme. This form was created by Theresa King © 2000

A few examples of a quatrain rhyming scheme are as follows:

#1 abab
#2 abba—envelope rhyme
#3 aabb#4 aaba, bbcd,
#4 ccdc, dddd—chain rhyme

Rictameter

Rictameter is a scheme similar to Cinquain. Starting your first line with a two syllable word, you then consecutively increase the number of syllables per line by two . i.e. 2 4 6 8 10, then down again, 8 6 4 2. Making the final line the same two syllable word you began with.

&****&

Poetry Glossary Page 8

Rondelet

The Rondelet is a French form consisting of a single septet with two rhymes and one refrain: AbAabbA. The capital letters are the refrains, or repeats. The refrain is written in tetra-syllabic or dimeter and the other lines are twice as lone- octasyllabic or tetrameter.

Senryu

Most popular definition, but there is more to senryu than meets the eye:
Senryu is an unrhymed Japanese verse consisting of 5 7 5 syllables in all. Senryu is usually written in the present tense and only references to some aspect of human nature or emotions.

Seventh Heaven

This form was created by Joseph Spence Sr © 10/21/2007 All rights reserved
The form is 7/11/7/11/7/11/7. The syllable count is 61. The first line has seven syllables, second eleven, third seven, fourth eleven, fifth seven, sixth eleven, and seventh seven. Rhyming is optional; however it's a plus. Any variation of the words "seven" or "heaven" must appear in the poem.

Somonka

A poem that resembles a tanka. It has 5, 7, 5, 7, 7 syllables but is written in 10 lines with a response in second stanza. A poet must write as the second person to write this style themselves or co-write with another person.

&****&

Poetry Glossary Page 9

Sonnet

A Sonnet is a poem consisting of 14 lines (iambic pentameter) with a particular rhyming scheme:

Example of a rhyming scheme:

#1 abab cdcd efef gg
#2 abba cddc effe gg
#3 abba abba cdcd cd

A Shakespearean (English) sonnet has three quatrains and a couplet, and rhymes abab cdcd efef gg.

An Italian sonnet is composed of an octave, rhyming abbaabba and a sestet, rhyming cdecde or cdcdcd, or in some variant pattern, but with no closing couplet.

Usually English and Italian Sonnets have 10 syllables per line, but Italian Sonnets can also have 11 syllables per line.

French sonnets follow in this same pattern, but normally have 12 syllables per line.

Swap Quatrain

The Swap Quatrain was created by Lorraine . Kanter _© 2004. Within the Swap Quatrain each stanza in the poem must be a quatrain (four lines) where the first line is reversed in the fourth line. In the addition, line 2 must rhyme with line 1, and line 3 must rhyme with line 4 and so on, BUT not repeat the same rhyming pattern on subsequent stanzas. Rhyme is AABB CCDD and so on.

&****&

Poetry Glossary Page 10

Tanka

Tanka is a classic form of Japanese poetry related to the haiku with five unrhymed lines of five, seven, five, seven, and seven syllables. (5, 7, 5, 7, 7)

Tetractys

Tetractys, a poetic form invented by Ray Stebbing, consists of at least 5 lines of 1, 2, 3, 4, 10 syllables (total of 20). Tetractys ca be written with more than
one verse, but must follow suit with an inverted syllable count. Tetractys can also be reversed and written 10, 4, 3, 2, 1.

Double... 1, 2, 3, 4, 10, 10, 4, 3, 2, 1 etc

Tree of Life

This form was created by Christina R Jussaume on 12/03/07. You begin with one syllagble until you reach 13 syllables. The next 6 lines have 4 syllables each. There is no rhyme. It should be center aligned to show shape of tree. This form should b e spiritual, or about something uplifting in content.

&****&

Poetry Glossary Page 11

Tina-Rhyme

This form was created by Chazz Combs. It' is a syllabic form. The syllable count is 2 3 6 7 9 13 11 9 7 6 3 and 2.

Wrapped Refrain

The Wrapped Refrain created by Jan Turner, consists of 2 stanzas of 6 lines each; Meter: 8 8 8 8 12 12 and Rhyme scheme is a, a, b, b, c, c

Refrain rule: In each stanza the first 4 syllables (Or 4 single syllable words) in the first line must be the last 4 syllables (or 4 single syllable words) at the end of the last line. This is what wraps each stanza with a repeated refrain; thus the Wrapped Refrain

Optional: The first stanza refrain and last stanza refrain can be joined (or loosely joined) together for the title of the poem

&****&

Christina's Other Books

ISBN-13: 978-1424168309

I found myself taking 'My Walk with Jesus' in poetry After I lost both of my parents before I forty years of age. By writing poetry I found relief from the grief. My poetry helped me to see the beauty given by God. The beauty I had seen all of my life I began to write about. This collection of poems expresses my faith. With God in my life I handled all things put before me. This collection is written with the essence of my heart and soul. These words I express with a sincere heart. Now won't you take this walk with me to see the beauty God has given all around us? Enjoy the beauty of rose gardens and magnificent sunsets as I bring them all to life within my poems. I felt peace as I wrote this collection and now this peace I will share with you. For more info about this or any other book by Christina visit her website at

www.poetesscrjussame.com

&****&

Amazing Pets & Animals
By
Christina R Jussaume

ISBN: 978-0-6151-8028-1

Published by Passion for Poetry Publishers:
This collection of poetry was inspired by all the loving pets I have had and still have. It is poetry stories of all the many different memories we did share together in love and harmony. I also have included some fantasy story poems about animals that both adults and children will enjoy. There are some fables within this collection with a moral that teaches values. I have also created a few new invented poetry styles. All of my poetry is inspired by God, my life and inspiration from my family and pets. To purchase any book or for more info visit either or both websites shown.

www.poetesscrjussaume.com

&****&

Passion for Poetry Publishers
(Other Books)

The Wizard, The Witch & Joe the Toe.
By
Patricia Ann Farnsworth-Simpson.

ISBN 978-0-6151-8027-4

A fantasy story about a deformed boy growing up tormented and neglected so that he is only fit to herd goats...Till one day he helps a lost old man who turns out to be a wizard that befriends him and turns him into a man of real good standing within the community...so that he gets a wife to have children.. but not before overcoming lots more trouble to both himself and the Wizard... plus the Wizard´s poor Dragon that is all created by an evil jealous Witch... eventually though happiness is found and like all good children's stories it ends with them all living happy ever after...

For more info visit the publishers website
at
www.pfppublishers.com

&****&

Jack the Lad
By
Patricia Ann Farnsworth-Simpson

ISBN: 978-0-6151-8415-9

This is a tale of how a boy and his Mother are evicted from the colliery house when his Dad dies. It is a story that shows how the young lad fights back to get a job and a home for his Mother so they never again have to sleep rough. It is a lovely story that will encourage kids to read more as they will find it absorbing and Adults will enjoy it too, especially if from a mining back ground.
For more info visit the publishers website at

www.pfppublishers.com

&****&

Tales of a Tiny Dog
By
Daveda Gruber

ISBN: 978-0-6151-8157-8

This book is in full color and has pictures of people and dogs that are a part of Daveda's enchanting life. Give the child in your life a real treat. Let them read and see the tales of a tiny dog name Lady Godiva. She is a chocolate teacup poodle that weighs four pounds, full grown; a small but mighty pup that will win many a heart!
      For more info visit the publishers website at

www.pfppublishers.com

&****&

More Snapshots
By
Daveda Gruber

ISBN: 978-0-6151-8648-1

This book is Daveda Gruber's follow up to "Snapshots ...a Blonde View". Daveda is a storyteller who can tell a story to rhyme that will capture the interest of anyone! Daveda takes you on a lighthearted journey from childhood to becoming a wife, sister, mother and friend. Come along, but hold on tight when you join Daveda, as she journeys through a unique life that is all her own!
For more info visit the publishers website at

www.pfppublishers.com

&****&

Passion For Poetry!

Contact E.Mail: p.f.p.publishers@gmail.com

www.ingramcontent.com/pod-product-compliance
Lightning Source LLC
Chambersburg PA
CBHW022133080426
42734CB00006B/345